Henry's Blog

CONTENTS

D1424330

Henry's Blog

Tada!

My life so far...

This is my BLOG for recording the proper grown-up life of me, Prince Henry, people. Just as soon as I start having one, obvs.

FYI

- I was born on 28 June 1491
- Older brother Arthur will be the next king, NOT ME
- I've got red hair

Pic of me and my family in 1502! ↑ That's me aged nearly 11 in front with a shield. My brother Arthur aged 16 is on my left, my dad Henry VII and mum Elizabeth of York are at the back. On my right is my kid sister Mary aged 6 and older sister Margaret aged 13.

Welcome to me

Who's who part 1: my rellies and rivals

My dad, Henry VII (Henry7)

My mum, Elizabeth of York

My brother, Arthur

My older sister, Margaret

My younger sister, Mary

Wife no. 1: Katherine of Aragon (KatyA)

Francis I of France (Frazza)

Chief Minister 1: Cardinal Thomas Wolsey (Wozza)

Henry's Blog

Me 2 B king

My life so far

When my dad married my mum, it finished like, EVIL quarrels between my dad's family (the Lancasters) and my mum's family (the Yorks), who both wanted to rule England. 👁

So my dad combined the family badges, a red rose and a white rose, to make the TUDOR ROSE. Then he stuck it all over the place to make sure everyone knew the Tudors were here to stay. TADA!

The deal

10 AUG 1501

09:31

    My brother Arthur is going to marry KatyA, a Spanish princess. They're like, not exactly loved-up. Dad fixed everything with King Ferdinand of Spain (KatyA's dad), when they were er, um, babies. That's how it's done, OK?

The marriage means England and Spain will be best mates. Which is good because Spain, being **MEGA** powerful, could zap England, like, into orbit. A big plus: KatyA comes with a MASSIVE dowry (cash and jewels and stuff).

The wedding

14 NOV 1501

12:30

    Official Amazing Day. VIPs stuffed inside St Paul's. People outside standing on roof-tops, etc, etc, to get a peek. Enter **ME** with KatyA dressed in a fab frock to meet Arthur at the altar. Q loads of trumpet fanfares. People of the Blog, **I GIVE YOU ARTHUR AND KATYA!** ➡

My big brother Arthur

My brain hurts

10:31

OMGOMGOMG!!!!! Arthur's only gone and **DIED!!!!!** That is totally hardcore. He was 15 and had only been married for 5 months. It was a 'sweating sickness' or something. Yeah, right, so they don't know. Well. Um. What they do know is I'll be **KING** when Dad dies! I hope this means I won't have to be sensible. I'll be the wisest, generousest, powerfullest, magnificentest king. Like, EVAH.

Big matterz

07:32

Anyway lookie, I'm almost 11. The parents are doing their 'WE MUST TALK ABOUT BEING KING' and I do nodding. And Dad wants me to marry KatyA. 'She's very pretty' which in the language of the PARENTS means 'We must remain friends with Spain. And we're not giving the dowry back.' Actually, KatyA is pretty cool so I'm like, luckily OK with that. ☺

Post a comment

 HENRY7

My son Arthur is DEAD. Life sucks.

 KATYA

So. Hello? What's going to happen to me?

 KING FERDI

I blame zose 'orrid cold castles of Inglaterra.

Just off 4 tennis.
B back soon.

Henry's Blog

My big day

My life so far

My dad died on 21 April 1509. Nothing gruesome – he just never got over the death of Arthur and then my mum, a year later. ☹

Loadz of people (me included), thought he was a stingy old king – but he's left me a well-run country, tons of money, totally amazing horses, several rubbish palaces and FIVE warships. Like, that's more than the mega kings of France and Spain! 😎

I am king

24 APR 1509

10:48

I'm almost 18 and I've been ~~proclaimed~~ like turned into king. So now there shall be some action! First up, I'm going to give Dad's zombie ministers the chop 'cos they don't like my big new plans. Then I'm going to marry KatyA. **GO ME!**

What's happening

21 JUN 1509

09:03

Today's **MY** day! It's all a bit mental what with the wedding ten days ago. Anyway, KatyA and I will ride out from the Tower of London to our coronation in Westminster Abbey. It's tradition, OK?

Post a comment

 JOE BLOGS

WOW!!!! The new King and Queen. Cool!

 LADY-IN-WAITING

OMG!!!! KatyA looked TOTALLY AMAZING dressed in white and Henry uber-cool in crimson and gold.

Me aged 18

23 JUN 1509

Action!

12:00

Now I'm king this is what I'm going to do:

👑 **FACT 1:** Hunt, eat, drink and partaaay!

👑 **FACT 2:** Joust with my mates (a sort of weirdo fight where we knock each other off our horses with giant poles but try not to KILL each other).

👑 **FACT 3:** Have lots of SONS to rule after me, obvs.

👑 **FACT 4:** Get Wozza to govern the country for me. Because, hello? It's boring.

PLZE DO NOT POINT OUT THAT I SHOULD BE CHOOSING MINISTERS, DISHING OUT WISE ADVICE, RULING PEOPLE AND GROWN-UP STUFF LIKE THAT, OK?

Things I'm lovin' right now

- Being King of England
- CHILLING
- KatyA

Annoyances

The TOWER OF LONDON is a bit minging 'cos the last king to make big improvements was Edward I who lived, like, zillions of years ago. Duh! Anyway, I'll live mostly in my other palaces and at best mates' cool houses. Whatevs.

Post a comment

 WOZZA

So what's in it for me? Like SERIOUS money and power!

Gotta go – I'm jousting at the Tower. B right back.

STATUS: SIGNING OUT

My life so far...

When I came to the throne six years ago in 1509, the kings of France and Spain and the Holy Roman Emperor were the most powerful rulers in Europe. They still are. GRRRRRRRRR!

Meanwhile, KatyA has had four babies. Total GLUMFACE. They all died including little Prince Henry who only lived for seven weeks. ☹ But the next baby will DEFINITELY BE A SON.

grrrr!

JAN 1515

Boys' stuff

12:10

You know what? I totally love cool stuff like big guns, forts and weapons. So it's TOTAL CRISIS that my armour is A BIT PANTS. What's worse is that other kings present me with fab armour made in their own workshops. They like to drop me in the poo, no? Anyway lookie, I'm going to get brilliant craftsmen to set up workshops in Greenwich to make the best armour EVAH. Ner!

SEPT 1515

A new suit of armour

10:14

So. Hello? I'm getting the most KRAZEE suit of armour. It's made of steel and decorated all over with saints, scary torture scenes, awesome executions, mermen, the Tudor rose, St George and the Dragon, my family badges, KatyA's family badges and love knot thingies. Woohoo!

and babies

"Oh no! it's a girl"

It's a princess

18 FEB 1516

14:00

KatyA has given birth to a baby girl. Well, that really, really sucks. **SHE PROMISED ME A SON.** (*bigsulks*)

21:29

Erm... actually the baby is quite sweet. Not so sweet as a baby prince, obvs. It's just that I *soooo* need a son to rule after me. That's the way it will always be, no?

22:30

Feeling less of a grotpot today. We'll name the baby Mary and marry her off to the young French Dauphin and get some lands back from France that way.

20 FEB 1516

11:13

So. Hello? All these foreign VIPs are congratulating me on the safe birth of Princess Mary. But I know they're *so* thinking and 'what a disappointment'. Well, it is. But what I'm saying is: 'It will be a son next time'. Let anyone who says otherwise be very, very careful. **Get my drift?**

Post a comment

EMPEROR MAXIMILIAN

Hi Henry. I'm sending you this gorgeous show helmet of fantastic craftsmanship.

Things to do

I want a helmet with MY face on it. Why don't you, like, design me one?

England vs

My life so far...

Over the last few years, I've WON, repeat, WON, a couple of battles in France. ☺ Frazza and Chaz (Charles V Emperor of the Holy Roman Empire), say that it would be quite useful to be best mates with me. So they've decided that what's cool for everyone and the future would be peace, not war.

Royal Celebrations

No event too big

www.uppakrusta-tudor.net

Peace, maybe?

7 MAY 1520

09:00

I've decided to make a big thing of this peace treaty stuff. So, like, I've told Wozza to fix it and BIG UP my magnificence, obvs.

14 MAY 1520

10:00

Frazza alert! He wants to be as magnificent as me! I've told Wozza **NO WAY!** Wozza fixed the meeting for 7-24 June to be held in France, but near Calais. Why? 'Cos Calais is ruled by me. Duh!

19 MAY 1520

08:55

Frazza wants the meeting held on a bit of France ruled by him. He's such a demanding twonk. OK, I'll get Wozza to fix the meeting halfway between the two places. ☹

21 MAY 1520

16:29

Plze order up loadz of wine, ginormous banquets, archery competitions, jousting, mock battles, jugglers, minstrels, fortune tellers, mock castles, fireworks, music, cute girls wearing fab clothes, cool knights (but not as cool as me, obvs). Spare no expense Wozza! **Let's partaaaay!**

France

Pic of ME about to meet Frazza

Post a comment

 WOZZA

OMG! Just got the bill for the Field of Cloth of Gold. Like, TOTALLY empty moneybags! Me in thinky mode: monasteries are, like, v. v. rich. A useful source of dosh, no?

Peace, I think not

24 JUN 1520

02:44

I'm blogging into the night. And I don't want anybody's opinion OK? The meeting (called the Field of Cloth of Gold 'cos the tents were made of gold cloth) was awesome. UNTIL I CHALLENGED FRAZZA TO A WRESTLING MATCH. He won. (But like, in a totally failing way.) AND EVERYBODY CLAPPED. Felt a total twonk. This does not spell peace to me. NO. NO. NO. **WOZZA WILL TAKE THE BLAME.**

Annoyances

- Frazza 'cos he beat me
- Wozza 'cos he's moaning about dosh
- KatyA 'cos she's too old to have more kidz
- All that expense and England and France are even less friendly now!

Going to bed now ☹

My life so far...

A summer's day 1524 at Hampton Court. Enter ME, all round babe magnet and fashion icon. The music stops. Heads turn. People faint. I am like duh! the most CHILLAX king in the history of 4evah! ☺ ☺ ☺

FYI

- I'm like much taller than most men at court
- I speak five languages
- I love to dance (OMG! My moves!)
- I'm a bit of a music freak
- And I LOVE sport especially hunting, hawking, wrestling, tennis, jousting, shooting and archery. Woo!

Check out this pic of me. Clicky click! ⬆ Not sure who painted it but he did a totally AMAZING job. Note plenty of heavy-metal bling, cool velvet jacketty thing with slashed sleeves and the sharp hat. How about the designer stubble? A bit of a dude, no? 😎

at right now

Who's who part 2: wives, children and ministers

Wife no. 2: Anne Boleyn (AnnieB)

Princess Mary: my daughter by KatyA

Princess Elizabeth: my daughter by AnnieB

Wife no. 3: Jane Seymour (Janie)

Prince Edward (Eddie): my son by Janie

Wife no. 4: Anne of Cleves (AnnieC)

Wife no. 5: Catherine Howard (Catz)

Wife no. 6: Kateryn Parr (KatP)

Chief Minister 2: Sir Thomas More (Mozza)

Chief Minister 3: Thomas Cromwell (Crommo)

Archbishop Cranmer (Archbish Crazza)

I want a

My life so far...

I've now been married to KatyA for 17 years. She has had six babies and the only one to survive is Princess Mary, who is now 10. I MUST HAVE A SON TO RULE AFTER ME.

Meanwhile, Wozza has become, like, SCARILY powerful! His palace at Hampton Court is LOADZ bigger than any of mine. 😠

Anne Boleyn

15 JUN 1526 *13:00*

Have I mentioned, erm... AnnieB? She was lady-in-waiting to the French queen for ages. But now she's rocked up to my court. Check out her pic. ➡

19 AUG 1526 *17:30*

AnnieB like, whoa, smoulder alert! I bet she could give me sons. Triplets probs. (*turnspink*)

11 OCT 1526 *19:05*

EEEEEEK! Global crush x zillions! AnnieB completely ignores that I'm, like, THE MEGA KING OF ENGLAND OF ALL TIME. Now she's gone off to live at her dad's castle. 😠

24 DEC 1526 *20:57*

I've written squillions of letters and ridden my fave horse at illegal speeds to see her. Like, she still won't say whether she wants to get it together with me or not. 🙁

divorce!

Total freakout

11:30

I gave AnnieB awesome jewels for New Year's Day. Now she says she totally loves me! WIN! BUT she quite massively won't have my babies **UNLESS. SHE. BECOMES. QUEEN. OF. ENGLAND.** 🙁

23:01

OMG!!!! What am I going to do about KatyA? Solution!!! KatyA was Arthur's widow, right? That MUST be against the law! Woooo! I'm not really married to KatyA at all! I'll get Wozza to fix a divorce – he's best mates with the Pope. 🙂

> Did you see...!
>
> Anne's such a street rat!
>
> I tell you it won't work
>
> woof!

Post a comment

 ANNIEB

Henry sweetikins, I *sooo* don't think wanting to be queenie is too much to ask.

 WOZZA

Happy New Year! If you're online, most excellent Pope, how about fixing Henry up with a divorce?

 THE POPE

NO WAY!

 KATYA

I AM THE QUEEN!

Quicky divorce? No problem!

www.freakytudorlawyers.co.uk

Henry's Blog

My fit new

My life so far…

After the Pope refused to give me a divorce, I split from the Roman Catholic Church and made myself the **SUPREME HEAD OF THE CHURCH OF ENGLAND.**

In 1530 I sacked Wozza for not fixing the divorce and accused him of TREASON (plotting against me which wasn't exactly true but kinda could've been). He died before I could have him executed. Shame. Mozza is my new chief minister.

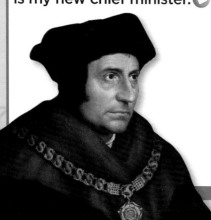

AnnieB is crowned queen

29 MAY 1533

13:00

In January, I secretly married AnnieB before I was, like, divorced from KatyA and her going NOOOOOOOO! Whatevs. Did I mention AnnieB is having a baby? **IT'S GOING TO BE A BOY.**

1 JUN 1533

16:25

AnnieB spent the night at the Tower before her coronation. I've had new apartments built for her. The Tower guns will fire BIG BANGS to make sure everyone knows AnnieB is my new queen. It's all quite yay. Except that not everyone thinks so. ☹

It's my big day!

Post a comment

 JOE BLOGS

Bring back Queen Katherine!

 MRS BLOGS

Anne Boleyn is *so* not our queen. Booooooo!

queen

My new palaces

10 MAY 1533

10:09

When I fell out with Wozza, I grabbed his palaces at Hampton Court and York Place (which I'm going to rename Whitehall). I'm building new apartments for AnnieB and a baby prince and adding squidsworths of bling.

Katherine to go

6 JUN 1533

14:00

OMG! KatyA is a twonk – she keeps banging on about being the real queen and still totally loving me, blah, blah. So I'm sending her to live miles away. Princess Mary will stay in London. So, no more mother-and-daughter time. Whatevs.

Princess Elizabeth

7 SEPT 1533

19:20

AnnieB has had the baby. IT'S ANOTHER GIRL. I CAN'T BELIEVE IT! What have I done to deserve this? I WANT A SON. AND I WANT ONE NOW!

Post a comment

ANNIEB

OMG!! It's a girl (*nail bites*) Next time lucky?

PRINCESS MARY

Ner to her!

KATYA

Ha! Ha!

FOREIGN VIP

Sooo sorry it wasn't a boy... again.

Annoyances

- AnnieB for not giving me a son
- Mozza for siding with the Pope
- KatyA for being all pleady
- Mary for being all 'the only true princess'

I vote

My life so far...

It's two years since I married AnnieB in 1532 and things have gone woes-makingly wrong. Mozza refused to agree to the divorce and the split from the Pope. So he was executed on Tower Hill TO SHOW WHAT HAPPENS TO PEOPLE WHO DON'T OBEY ME.

Crommo is my new Chief Minister. AnnieB has had two more babies who didn't survive. It's scarily like it was with KatyA! (*darkthoughts*)

Time for action

JAN 1535

15:35

I've just had a word with Crommo about, um, er, AnnieB's future. Or non future as it happens.

Me: I'm feeling scary.

Crommo: What kind of scary?

Me: Umm. Tricky to say. But I don't think it'll surprise anyone.

Crommo: Dish the dirt then.

Me: Think I made a mistake marrying AnnieB...

Crommo: Yeah, well...

Me: I think she used, like, witchyness to trap me?

Crommo: Whoooooa!

Me: Yeah, she's a witch. That's why I haven't got a son. I'm thinking AnnieB's got to go.

Crommo: Divorce, no?

Me: Something a bit quicker.

Crommo: Eeeek! That is TOTALLY hardcore!

AnnieB off

FEB 1535

Jane Seymour

14:59

Anyway, lookie, I've spotted the sister of one of my mates. I'll post Janie's pic. She's a bit dorky - not all shouty and bitey like AnnieB – which is good. I *sooo* couldn't stand that again. I want peace and quiet and my oldest and dearest friends back.

Shocking!

Post a comment

ANNIEB

U R A TOTAL LOVE RAT!

Secret thoughtz

I'm blogging for my mental health. I've accused AnnieB of seeing ex-boyfriends and plotting against me. (Which isn't exactly true but like, it sort of could be.) I'm sending her to ~~pongy dungeons crawling with big hairy rats~~ comfy rooms in the Tower.

Things to do

How will Henry TOTALLY get rid of AnnieB? Will he:

- Behead her with a sharp sword?
- Execute her with a blunt axe?

Answer: GO TO PAGE 32

Gotta go 4 a game of tennis. B right back.

STATUS: SIGNING OUT

My life so far...

1536 was, like, WEIRD. First KatyA died. ~~Relief!~~ Two days after AnnieB's erm, execution, Crommo said that the marriage wasn't legal anyway. Duh! Eleven days later, I married Janie. Then the Pope hinted he MIGHT talk to me now that AnnieB was, um... dead. But I *sooo* think not.

off with the spots

Wife no. 3

FEB 1537

18:04

Woo! Janie is expecting a baby! ☺ I'm building new apartments for her at Hampton Court with rooms for a prince, obvs. He will have a special rocking room for his cradle and his own kitchen. Yeah, and I've made sure that AnnieB's leopard badges are changed to Janie's panther ones. Eezee-peezee – just blitz the spots!

I'm waiting...

11 OCT 1537

15:37

I'm totally kerknackered. I've been staying up all night awaiting news of the BABY.

It's a boy!

12 OCT 1537

19:43

OMGOMGOMG!!!! TOTALLY AWESOME NEWS. IT'S A BOY! IT'S A BOY! IT'S A BOY! Woooohooo! Let the celebrations begin! Church bells will ring out, bonfires will be lit, there will be street parties and like, a zillion gun salute at the Tower for my SON AND HEIR. It will be total mental madcakes!

at last!

Prince Edward

15 OCT 1537

12:02

Prince Edward (Eddie) was christened in total awesome magnificence in the Chapel Royal at Hampton Court. Eighty of the most important men in England led the procession. Princess Mary is his godmother and little Elizabeth carried the christening cloth. Archbish Crazza did the religious bits and knights announced his royal titles: son and heir to the King of England, Duke of Cornwall, Prince of Wales and Earl of Chester. I'm posting a pic of the Chapel Royal NOW.

Post a comment

 CROMMO

I promoted Janie's rellies to earls and stuff.

 DOC

The baby is doing fine but Janie has suddenly gone down with a fever or something. Better organise prayers for her.

 CRAZZA

The prayers worked. Janie is feeling better, yay!

DOC

Is Janie better? No, she is not. She is worse.

 CRAZZA

OMGOMGOMG!!!!! Janie is dead.

If anyone's looking 4 me, I'm UNAVAILABLE.

STATUS: SIGNING OUT

My life so far...

It's been two years since Janie died in 1537. I was in need of BIG HUGS so Crommo picked out a few princessy types to cheer me up. Some of them are saying no to me 'cos my wives always come to a sticky end. Yeah, like, that's *sooo* not fair. I mean, KatyA, was well past her sell-by-date. AnnieB got in the way of a sharp sword. And poor Janie... Well, hardly my fault.

Single again

20 JAN 1538

13:20

I'm asking cute little Christina of Denmark what the chances are of her and me getting it together. Her husband died, like, three years ago. So, hey! No problemo!

27 FEB 1539

14:05

Christina said NO! Something about keeping her head? Whatevs. Crommo tells me the Duke of Cleves has got two cute sisters. I'll send over Holbein, my fave artist, to paint their pix. And then choose the best looking babe. Yay!

30 AUG 1539

15:13

OMG! the pic of AnnieC is TOTALLY GORGEOUS. Check it out now plze. Look, Dukey, not only would AnnieC make a great looking queen but, like, you and me could gang up against Frazza, no?

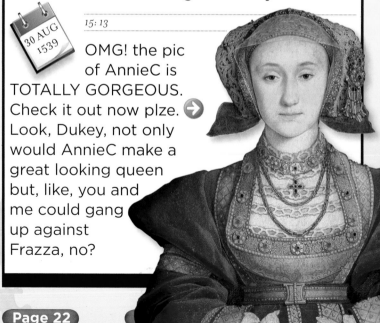

marriage

I'm Henry the Eighth I am

31 DEC 1539

Anne of Cleves

15:44

AnnieC is on her way from Germany! I'm checking her out before she gets to London. IN. DISGUISE. Then I'll pull it off and AnnieC will see ME. THE. KING. I'll schmooze her with fancy furs and bling. And it will be happy ever after. Tada!

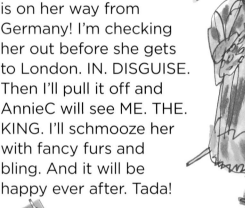

11:05

Well, that was like, THE ALL TIME BIGGEST DISASTER. AnnieC is so totally not my type. Doesn't speak a word of English, she's not into music, her clothes are total mingwear and she's got stupid hair. Noooooooo! ☹

Crommo says I must marry AnnieC 'cos if not it'll cause a BIG INCIDENT. Shame 'cos I've just spotted a cool babe. Right. So I'm going to divorce AnnieC asap. Yeah, I know she can read this but I don't care. And, Crommo if you are reading this: BE VERY AFRAID.

Secret thoughtz

OK, no wife so I'm going to play with my FAB new clock ⬆ which I'm having built for Hampton Court. It's got loadzzz of OMG features like it shows the time, month and day, the position of the sun in the zodiac and the age of the moon. And it will show the time of high water at London Bridge. Why? 'Cos it's kinda useful when I travel to Hampton Court by river. Duh!

Post a comment

 ANNIEC

I sink I like Henrich v much. But he act v strange, jah? ☹

Henry's Blog

Invasion

My life so far...

When Wozza suggested a few years ago that monasteries might be a good source of dosh, and could be, erm, 'helped to modernise', I like thought WIN! So in 1536, I ordered the small monasteries to close. And executed a few abbots who, like, objected. This didn't go down too well with the Pope who ganged up with the French and Germans and threatened to invade England. Like, total hardcore!

OUT YOU GO!

Little Eddie

19:49

Here's a pic of Eddie aged about 2. Check out his totally cool hat! Already a fashion icon just like ME.

Large monasteries to close

19:49

Crommo is doing a totally amazing job of closing all the larger and richer monasteries. His hit squads order the buildings to be stripped of all the valuable stuff. And all the monks and nuns are sent packing. End of!!

Post a comment

 CROMMO

We had 800 monasteries in 1536. By next year they will have all gone. (*highfives*)

ABBOT

So. Hello? Like, who will be feeding the poor, caring for the sick and praying for your soul? Not that you've got one.

alert!

Loadz of dosh

16 MAY 1540

08:03

Eeeeeek! Scarily tough? I think not. The monasteries were all bad anyway (not exactly true, but sort of could be, OK?). I'm selling off land and buildings to my mates as rewards for sticking with me through all the tricky stuff with the Pope. Now I've got money to build more palaces, forts – and schools. So WIN all round except for monks and nuns. Whatevs.

At war

3 JUN 1540

12:12

News reached me last year that France was going to invade. OMG. TOTAL. CRISIS. So I've been making extra scary plans to KEEP FRAZZA OUT.

- I've got hundreds of men working on massive forts.
- I've ordered loadz of men to train for fighting.
- I've ordered loadz more weapons and ammo.
- I've upgraded my fab warships.

Secret thoughtz

I'm getting a top military engineer over from Germany to design the forts. They will be *so* not like the Tower. They'll have low, thick walls to withstand a hammering from big guns. Stuff like this doesn't come cheap. But I've got the money now. Woo!

Post a comment

FRAZZA

Enri – leeetle change of le plan. You vereee lucky. We will not invade this time. Later maybe...

Gotta go. Just off for a wrestling match. B right back.

STATUS: SIGNING OUT

I marry a

My life so far...

I divorced AnnieC as soon as possible. Luckily for her she saw sense and decided not to make a fuss. I gave her some palaces and stuff and said she could come to Court anytime she liked (provided she warned me so I could be, like, unavailable).

People call her 'the king's sister'. Well, it's a zillion times better than the king's wife. Of course, her brother, the Duke of Cleves isn't too cool about it. Whatevs.

such a pretty neck

Catherine Howard

1 JUL 1540   *09:47*

Anyway lookie, I'm in love. Yes, ok, AGAIN. Babe of the moment is Catz. She's 17 and I'm ~~um... 3 times her age~~, a wee bit older. The walking stick I use is just for show, OK?

I'm posting a pic of Catz wearing the fabuloso jewels I've given her. ➡

28 JUL 1540   *10:48*

People of the Blog, in seven days time Catz and I are getting married. Of all my wives I love Catz the best. It's *sooo* for real this time.

Post a comment

 CATZ

OMG! The King has fallen for me! Scary or thrilling? Or possibly both? Whatevs. Thnx for the sparkles, daddio. ☺

  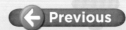

teenager

Betrayed!

2 NOV 1541

21:30

OMGOMGOMG!!!!! I was in the Chapel Royal when I found a note from Crazza saying that Catz has been cheating on me – like for MONTHS. NOOOOOOOOO! I swear I'll cut of her pretty little head myself!!!!

Catz for the chop

15 NOV 1542

09:30

He's not in

Catz like TOTALLY deceived me. Mega hardcore humiliation! I had her arrested but she managed to dodge her guards. I could hear her screaming and pleading for her life when I was in the Chapel Royal but I blocked my ears and had the doors locked. She'll pay the price. **NO ONE TRASHES THE KING OF ENGLAND, OK?**

Post a comment

 ANON 1

Have you heard that Catz has been meeting like, you know, other men? Mind you, you can't blame her can you? Fancy having to kiss that stinking great hulk!

 ANON 2

Yeah, she's been seeing old boyfriends, apparently. SHUSH and Double SHUSH!

 CATZ

PLEEEEZE! PLEEEEZE! PLEEEEZE! PLEEEEZE! I can explain...

 ANNIEC

Henry married Catz only three weeks after he divorced me. So. Hello? Who's complaining? I didn't lose my head, right?

Wife no. 6–

My life so far...

Catz was taken to the Tower on 11 February 1542 and told she'd be beheaded the next day. According to the Captain of the Tower, she asked to see the block so she could have a sort of dress rehearsal. I suppose she thought she'd look cool if she knew where to put her neck. **MEMO TO ME: DON'T MARRY ANOTHER TEENAGER.**

Kateryn Parr

14 DEC 1542

10:56

OMG I've just heard from twonkface AnnieC. She keeps banging on about wanting to meet up with me again blah, blah. That is *sooo* not going to happen. Anyway, I've got my eye on KatP. ➔

Wedding day. Again

12 JUL 1543

13:58

Today I'm marrying KatP at Hampton Court. She's 31 and twice widowed. I'm 52 and still a bit of a DUDE. KatP, erm... was about to marry Sir Thomas Seymour, Janie's younger brother. But she couldn't refuse the King. When Sir Thomas knew I was after her, he quietly disappeared. Very wise. ~~Otherwise he could have found himself like, without a head.~~

a good friend

My children

12 JUL 1543

10:19

KatP is a good wifey. She gets on well with Princess Mary who is, ahem, only four years younger than her. And she's kind to Princess Elizabeth who is now 10 and to Eddie who is 6. Even more important, she can look after me now I'm getting on a bit. I, um... think it's going to be all lovely huggy and cosiness from now on. 🖤

Into battle

1 JUL 1545

11:51

The French invasion fleet has set sail for England – 'cos we captured Boulogne a year ago, probs. Wooo! I love a fight. I'm travelling down to the south coast to see my fave warship the *Mary Rose.* I've had her fitted out with loadz of amazing big-hitting cannon. I'll watch her sail into battle and blast the French out of the water. Yay! 🙂

DISASTER

19 JUL 1545

13.46

OMG!OMG! Noooooooooo! The *Mary Rose* has only gone and capsized and sunk in front of my very eyes!

Post a comment

 MARY

KatP is really nice. She's got totally cool shoes.

 ELIZABETH

KatP is *sooo* not a stepmonster.

 EDDIE

I love KatP, too!

 FOREIGN VIP

Well, this makes a change from divorce and um, chopping people's heads off.

If anyone is looking 4 me, I'm on my way back from the south coast.

STATUS: SIGNING OUT ✕

Not feeling

My life so far...

The last few years have been a bit madcakes what with Frazza threatening to invade. And I *sooo* don't want any more children now. Eddie is my heir and KatP has persuaded me to allow Mary and Elizabeth to rule after me. If Eddie should die young (v. v. unlikely), first Mary and then Elizabeth will become queen. But hey, that won't happen. England has never had a queen, right?

Happy families

13 APR 1546   *10:00*

So anyway, I've had this pic painted with me, Janie and Eddie in the middle. Mary is on the left and Elizabeth on the right. It will hang in Whitehall Palace so that everyone can see it. I KNOW JANIE HAS BEEN DEAD FOR YEARS, DUH! but I want to make sure THAT EVERYONE KNOWS that I believe that MY ONLY TRUE WIFE was Janie, 'cos she gave me my heir, Eddie.

Tired now

28 JUN 1546   *07:30*

It's my birthday today. I'm 55. But life SUCKS. My legs are very ouchy and I get big hurt headaches. But the wheelchair is JUST FOR SHOW. Here's my pic. Still a dude eh?

too good...

Remember me?

16:45

I've been ~~lying in bed~~ out riding thinking about my great achievieness:

Wives and children · Navy and schools · Palaces and forts

👑 **FACT 1:** I've made a great navy and built modern forts.

👑 **FACT 2:** I've built schools and colleges (but only for boys, obvs).

👑 **FACT 3:** I've got over 50 palaces and decorated them with work by great artists.

ANY RUMOURS THAT I WAS A TYRANT AND WIFE KILLER IS A CLUNKY GREAT LIE PUT ABOUT BY PEOPLE WHO DO NOT UNDERSTAND ME.

OK, OK so I'm very, very sick. I don't want to spend New Year with my rellies. I'm going to Whitehall to be ill in peace. I'm worse 'cos my doctors keep poking me around. They go: 'How's the old leg, sir?' **I'm dying you twonk!** Right now, I do not want to think about KatP, or my children, or my friends – if I've got any left, obvs.

Post a comment

DR OWEN

King Henry VIII died on 28 January 1547 at Whitehall. He was ~~like a giant, stinky, beached whale~~ peaceful in death. He didn't want to say goodbye to anyone, not even his wife and children. Henry will be buried in St George's Chapel in Windsor Castle next to his wife Janie, as he wished.

KATP

I'm thinking I'm going to marry Sir Thomas Seymour like NOW and invite Elizabeth to live with us. I'VE SURVIVED! Wooo! 🙂 🙂 🙂

EDDIE

I'm KING now. OMG! 🙂

Henry's Blog

More 4 U

Want to know more about Henry and his palaces?

The Tower of London

Lots of my ancient rellies stayed here, built on bits and made improvements. And of course AnnieB, Catz and loadz of people (including some, erm... one-time friends) who refused to see things my way, were imprisoned, or executed here.
For opening times and details of special events visit: www.hrp.org.uk

Hampton Court Palace

This is one of my fave palaces. You can see the Great Hall, the kitchens, my fab astronomical clock, the Chapel Royal and the badges of my six wives. Under Anne Boleyn's gateway, you can even see my initials still entwined with AnnieB's – which a poxy craftsman failed to chisel out!
For opening times and details of special events visit: www.hrp.org.uk

Further reading

Tower Power: Tales from the Tower of London, Power Palace: Tales from Hampton Court and *Kings and Queens: A Little Book of Rulers*
Available from all Historic Royal Palaces shops and online at www.hrp.org.uk

Answer P19:
I granted AnnieB's wish to be executed with a sword. She thought it was nobler than the block and axe.